Creativity
in Statecraft

CREATIVITY
·IN·
STATECRAFT

by Arthur Schlesinger, Jr.

Library of Congress   Washington   1983

OCCASIONAL PAPERS OF THE COUNCIL OF SCHOLARS
NO. I

Library of Congress Cataloging in Publication Data

Schlesinger, Arthur Meier, 1917–
   Creativity in statecraft.

   (Occasional papers of the Council of Scholars; no. 1)
   Includes bibliographical references.
   1. State, The.   2. Statesmen.   3. Creative ability.
I. Title.   II. Series.
JC325.S29   1983   320   82-24917
ISBN 0-8444-0418-7

Designed by John Michael

Preface

THE COUNCIL OF SCHOLARS

of the Library of Congress was established in 1980 to accomplish the following tasks: to serve as a link between the Library of Congress and the world of scholarship and to advise the Librarian of Congress on ways to sustain and strengthen this connection; to survey the Library's collections to ensure that they can support the most ambitious scholarly activity in all fields; and to deliberate periodically on large issues in the world of ideas and to prepare an inventory of knowledge of these issues. The inventory of knowledge is intended to inform the widest possible audience about what is known on a topic and about what aspects of the topic require further research and exploration.

The inaugural meeting of the council — held November 19-20, 1980, with the support and cooperation of the Carnegie Foundation for the Advancement of Teaching and the Standard Oil Company of California — was the occasion for a symposium on creativity, the first topic in the council's inventory of knowledge. Papers on various aspects of creativity were delivered and discussed. The council continued to investigate the subject at subsequent meetings, and eventually distilled its findings into a pamphlet, Creativity: A Continuing Inventory of Knowledge *(Washington: Library of Congress, 1981).*

In addition to its inventory of knowledge, the council is introducing a series of occasional papers by its members. The first of these, presented by Arthur Schlesinger, Jr., at the November 1980 Symposium on Creativity, is an analysis of creativity as applied to the field of statecraft. Future papers will cover a wide variety of topics within areas of sustained interest to the council. We hope that the public will welcome the opportunity to learn more about the council's investigations.

JAMES H. HUTSON
Executive Secretary

CREATIVITY

· IN ·

STATECRAFT

Creativity in Statecraft

It is with diffidence that I introduce a dubious topic into this otherwise elegant symposium. "Creativity in Science," "Creativity in the Arts" — these are quite obviously *subjects*. Creativity as a notion applies easily and inevitably to science and the arts. It is also applicable to political philosophy; one thinks at once of Plato, Aristotle, Hobbes, Locke, Montesquieu, Rousseau, Marx. But "Creativity in Statecraft"? in the practical conduct of government? Statecraft rarely expresses the soaring human spirit. It is at bottom an elemental necessity imposed on people when they weary of the war "of every man against every man"[1] and try to live together in orderly community. The primary function of statecraft is preservation, not innovation. At first glance, applying the notion of creativity to so rude a concern seems fanciful, if not scandalous. This may be why, until this symposium, "Creativity in Statecraft" has been an almost unknown subject.

i

What is creativity about? It is, let us say, the capacity for nontrivial innovation — for discovering significant and qualitatively distinct ways of doing things or of looking at the world.[2] In science and art the impulse to create issues typically in artifacts — experiments, equations, theories, paintings, poems, statues, sonatas. Such artifacts provide aesthetic delight — i.e., are ends in themselves — and at the same time enlarge the meaning of experience. Creative work thereby strengthens the ability of men and women to endure, make sense of, analyze, master, change a world that has appeared remorselessly in flux at least since Heraclitus found that he could not step twice into the same stream. Creativity implies that leap in imagination and understanding which enables individuals to achieve dignity and purpose in a universe where whirl is king.

The question arises whether creativity is a general phenomenon characterized by a common structure, or whether its character varies from one field to another. I would like to venture the hypothesis that creative processes across the board reveal, if not a common structure, at least a number of common features.

Let me, for purposes of illustration, offer a list of qualities that might be required for creative statecraft — a list taken, with the supporting quotations, from a famous commentator on the French Revolution. The first requirement on the list is Observation, "the ability to observe with accuracy things as they are in themselves," to know "whether the things depicted be actually present . . . or have a place only in the memory." Next, Reflection, which teaches "the value of actions, images, thoughts, and feelings; and assists the sensibility in perceiving their connection with each other." Then Imagination, "to modify, to create, and to associate"; then Invention; and finally Judgment, "to decide how and where, and in what degree, each of these faculties ought to be exerted; so that the less shall not be sacrificed to the greater; nor the greater, slighting the less, arrogate to its own injury, more than its due." These qualities, raised to the highest level make for genius, "the only proof [of which] is, the act of doing well what is worthy to be done, and what was never done before. . . . Genius is the introduction of a new element into the intellectual universe."

Now the introduction of a new element into the intellectual universe is a dangerous venture. Genius habitually provokes resistance. This commentator mentioned the problems encountered "in breaking the bonds of custom, in overcoming the prejudices of false refinement, and displacing the aversions of inexperience." Indeed, he himself, though later generations found his contributions lucid and straightforward, was angrily denounced by his contemporaries as pretentious, obscure, and incomprehensible.

You have already guessed that I am quoting, not at all from a discourse on statecraft, but rather from Wordsworth's Preface to the 1815 edition of his poems, where the onetime enthusiast for the French Revolution was considering "the powers requisite for the production of poetry."[3] His analysis suggests that creativity in politics draws on similar powers and risks similar rebuffs.

Wordsworth also understood how in the end genius conquers resistance. Here too his counsel applies to statecraft. "If there be one conclusion," he wrote, "more forcibly pressed upon us than another by the review which has been given of the fortunes and fate of poetical Works, it is this — that every author, as far as he is great and at the same time *original,* has had the task of *creating* the taste by which he is to be enjoyed.... To create taste is to call forth and bestow power."[4] Creativity is thus not simply genius at work in solitude but rather a complex and subtle relationship between the active sensibility of the creator and the latent sensibilities of his audience. Wordsworth survived while the critics who blackguarded him are forgotten because he, not they, created the sensibility of the future.

So the literary model at least offers certain key elements involved in creativity in both poetry and politics — observation, reflection, imagination, invention, judgment, originality, resistance by the orthodox, vindication by posterity.

ii

There are evident differences between the creative process in science and art and the creative process in statecraft.

One is the question of timing. We are all familiar with the slow, exasperating, unpredictable progress from "incubation" to "illumination" that marks creation in mathematics, say, or literature. Henri Poincaré calls "sudden illumination" the "manifest sign of long, unconscious prior work. The role of this unconscious work in mathematical invention appears to me incontestable."[5] Henry James talked about his custom of dropping an idea "into the deep well of unconscious cerebration, not without the hope, doubtless, that it might eventually emerge from that reservoir ... with a firm iridescent surface and a notable increase of weight."[6] "You must develop your ideas without tension or violence," said Gide. "And sometimes it does not come at once. You have to wait. This requires infinite patience. It's no good to seize hold of the idea against its will; it then seems so surly that you wonder what attracted you to it."[7]

The artist, even though his success ultimately depends on creating the taste by which he is enjoyed, still creates by himself, in his own time, subject to his own discipline. He makes his own choices, vibrates to his own iron string, marches to his own drummer. The scientist may use assistants in experiments and collaborators on papers, but his acts of pure creation are as lonely as those of painter or poet. As Lord Bryce, both scholar and statesman, wrote with unconcealed envy: "Dante in the sylvan solitudes of Fonte Avellana, Cervantes and Bunyan in the enforced seclusion of a prison, Hegel so wrapt and lost in his speculations that, taking his manuscript to the publisher in Jena on the day of the great battle, he was surprised to see French soldiers in the street; these are the types of the men and conditions which give birth to thoughts that occupy future generations."[8]

Like a long-legged fly upon the stream
His mind moves upon silence.

Science and art cannot be hurried. Statecraft is always under the clock. The statesman is the victim of emergency, the slave of crisis, and, even in tranquil times, the servant of deadlines. He must often seize ideas against their will and apply them without knowledge of consequences. He operates typically in "chronic obscurity"—the phrase General Marshall used to mention as characteristic of battlefield decisions, where one never quite knew how many troops the enemy had or where they were; one hardly knew where one's own troops were. Worse, the statesman often confronts situations in which, if he waits too long to be absolutely sure what the facts are, he may lose the opportunity to control developments. "When the scope for action is greatest," Henry Kissinger has observed, "knowledge on which to base such action is limited or ambiguous. When knowledge becomes available, the ability to affect events is usually at a minimum. In 1936, no one could know whether Hitler was a misunderstood nationalist or a maniac. By the time certainty was achieved, it had to be paid for with millions of lives."[9] Tocqueville said it shorter: "A democracy can obtain truth only as the result of experience; and many nations may perish while they are awaiting the consequences of their errors."[10]

The statesman must accept not only deadlines but also an exigent environment. He is forever coming to terms with others. Even totalitarianism involves jostling forces, argument, and adjustment, if only at the top. In a democratic polity the dialectic of compromise prevails all the way down. While artists and scientists reject compromise, march ahead on their own and bet on the consent of the future, statesmen require consent *now* if they are to achieve anything at all. Stendhal expected vindication in a century; Napoleon had to vindicate himself at once, or he was nothing. The artist, the scientist, have time and space; the statesman has little enough of either.

Statecraft, rushed on by crisis, acting on incomplete knowledge, under constant pressure to win consent, demands and develops qualities rather different from those nourished in creative solitude. "I have heard men who had gone from a quiet life into politics," wrote Bryce, "complain that they found their thinking powers wither, and that while they became far more expert in getting up subjects and speaking forcibly and plausibly, they found it harder and harder to form sound general views and penetrate beneath the superficialities of the newspaper and the platform."[11] "The true leader of men," said Woodrow Wilson, who, like Bryce, was both scholar and statesman, "is equipped by lacking certain sensibilities which the literary man, when analyzed, is found to have as a chief part of his make-up. . . . The motives which [political leaders] urge are elemental; the morality which they seek to enforce is large and obvious; the policy they emphasize, purged of all subtlety."[12]

Creativity in statecraft, then, shares common features with creativity in science and art. But there are also notable differences in the character of the process and above all in the quality of the product. Science and art are "possible" professions in the sense of Freud's list of the three "impossible" professions, those "in which one can be sure beforehand of achieving unsatisfying results" — education, psychoanalysis, and government.[13] "There is wonderfully little invention in the world," Bryce observed, "and perhaps least of all has been shown in the sphere of political institutions."[14] Measured by the standards of art and science, creativity in statecraft is impure, meager, forlorn. Still creativity in statecraft has its own purposes and therefore must be judged, to a degree at least, by its own standards.

iii

The purpose of creativity in statecraft is to find the means of orderly community in a world condemned to everlasting change. Bacon wrote long ago, "He that will not apply new remedies must expect new evils; for time is the greatest innovator."[15] Time's winged chariot has been hurrying faster than ever in the centuries since Bacon. The result in modern times is a permanent gap between existing institutions and an environment forever in motion. "Institutions," wrote Veblen, "are products of past process, are adapted to past circumstances, and are therefore never in full accord with the requirements of the present. In the nature of the case, this process of selective adaptation can never catch up with the progressively changing situation. . . . Each successive situation of the community in its turn tends to obsolesce as soon as it is established."[16] Or, as Bryce defined the problem of American statecraft in 1888, "In a country so full of change and movement as America, new questions are always coming up and must be answered. New troubles surround a government, and ways must be found to escape from them; new diseases attack the nation, and have to be cured. The duty . . . is to face these, to find answers and remedies."[17]

The search for remedy requires intellectual analysis and institutional invention. It requires most of all an instinct for the future. It demands the quality known grandly as "vision," by which is meant a sense both of the way the world is going and of the direction in which the statesman must carry his country. "True statecraft," said Tocqueville, calls for a "clear perception of the way society is evolving, an awareness of the trends of mass opinion and an ability to forecast the future."[18]

Among Americans no one perceived the dilemmas created by remorseless change more clearly than Henry Adams. Adams was born in 1838 in a society still run by a patrician elite based on the professions. "Lawyers, physicians, professors, merchants were classes, and acted not as individuals, but as though they were clergymen and each profession were a church." They "guided public opinion, but were little guided by it." Politics "offered no difficulties"; social perfection was also sure; no one foresaw radical change.[19]

But the nineteenth century, as Adams soon recognized, was preeminently a century of radical change. The accelerating explosion of science and technology discharged vast new energies into an unprepared society. "The world did not double or treble its movement between 1800 and 1900," as Adams wrote in 1909, "but, measured by any standard known to science . . . the tension and vibration and volume and so-called progression of society were fully a thousand times greater in 1900 than in 1800."[20] Everything buckled as society plunged headlong into the uncharted age of modern technology. Old elites were swept aside. The education young Adams received at Harvard in the 1850s proved useless; it stood, he decided, "nearer the year 1 than to the year 1900"; and he spent the rest of his life in a quest for an education that would suit the new age — that would "lessen the obstacles, diminish the friction, invigorate the energy and . . . train minds to react, not at haphazard, but by choice, on the lines of force that attract their world."[21]

In statecraft the old certitudes were equally irrelevant. In Washington in 1860: "the few people who thought they knew something were more in error than those who knew nothing." By 1870: "American society had outgrown most of its institutions." The system of 1789 was obsolete, and nine-tenths of political energies were now "wasted on expedients to piece out—to patch—or, in vulgar language, to tinker—the political machine as often as it broke down." Every historian, Adams said, must "put to himself the question: How long could such-or-such an outworn system last?" For Adams, "The political dilemma was as clear in 1870 as it was likely to be in 1970.... The sum of political life was, or should have been, the attainment of a working political system. Society needed to reach it. If moral standards broke down, and machinery stopped working, new morals and machinery of some sort had to be invented."[22]

This is the perennial mission of modern statecraft: to keep institutions and values sufficiently abreast of the accelerating velocity of history to give society a chance of managing the energies, and degradation thereof, let loose by science and technology on a hapless world. The objective remains the attainment of a working political system.

iv

Now it may be well to place creativity in statecraft in relation to the activity known as leadership. Obviously leadership is essential to make creativity effective. But leadership need not per se be creative. Leadership means no more than the ability to mobilize masses of people toward a given end. One may note here James MacGregor Burns's useful distinction between *transactional* and *transforming* leadership. Transactional leadership in Burns's definition mobilizes people by arranging exchanges of benefits between leaders and followers. Transforming leadership penetrates much deeper, carrying both leaders and followers to new levels of motivation and morality. Burns himself writes "higher" levels of motivation and morality, thereby denying transforming power to Hitler and Stalin. Requiring transforming leadership to be "moral" equates transforming leadership to some degree with creativity; but this identification seems to me to do less than justice to the force of Burns's own distinction.[23] People can be transformed for the worse as well as for the better.

Moreover, the emphasis on the need for transforming leaders to "address themselves to followers' wants, needs, and other motivations, as well as to their own"[24] tilts the theory perhaps in an unduly subjective direction. Creativity in statecraft has to do only secondarily with a subjective fit to internal, personal needs; it has to do primarily with an objective fit to external, social needs. Its concern is the provision of remedies, and the problems it attacks are essentially not those of the tremulous psyche within but of the creaky structure without.

Creativity in statecraft, in short, involves thought. It is a kind of problem-solving, though, we may agree with Herbert A. Simon, "a special kind." Successfully dividing 32 by 8 is problem-solving but hardly creative (at least not after the first primeval mathematician figured out how to do it). Simon sees "creative thinking" as marked by four salient characteristics:

1. The product of the thinking has novelty and value (either for the thinker or for his culture).
2. The thinking is unconventional, in the sense that it requires modification or rejection of previously accepted ideas.
3. The thinking requires high motivation and persistence, taking place either over a considerable span of time (continuously or intermittently) or at high intensity.
4. The problem as initially proposed was vague and ill-defined, so that part of the task was to formulate the problem itself.[25]

Creativity in statecraft is dependent therefore on the generation of ideas. Now, as Woodrow Wilson pointed out, ideas may suffer in the process by which they filter through politics into society. They may lose weight, form, color and emerge simplified and vulgarized in versions hardly recognizable to their originators. Nonetheless, ideas are in the end all that matter. "Indeed," as Keynes famously said, "the world is ruled by little else. Practical men, who believe themselves to be quite exempt from any intellectual influences, are usually the slaves of some defunct economist. Madmen in authority, who hear voices in the air, are distilling their frenzy from some academic scribbler of a few years back. . . . Soon or late, it is ideas, not vested interests, which are dangerous for good or evil."[26]

V

In statecraft as in art and science, ideas may be accepted by multitudes but they are originated by individuals. "The notion that a people can run itself and its affairs anonymously," as William James has observed, "is now well known to be the silliest of absurdities. Mankind does nothing save through initiatives on the part of inventors, great or small, and imitation by the rest of us — these are the sole factors in human progress. Individuals of genius show the way, and set the patterns, which common people then adopt and follow."[27]

Sir Karl Popper has warned us that "most investigations into the psychology of creative thought are pretty barren."[28] Still it may not be useless to consider the process by which people are driven to have new ideas. One must say *driven,* because habit and routine are easier than thought, and it requires extreme provocation to force people to think afresh. James has provided the classic account of the way in which we settle into new opinions.

> The individual has a stock of old opinions already, but he meets a new experience that puts them to a strain. Somebody contradicts them; or in a reflective moment he discovers that they contradict each other; or he hears of facts with which they are incompatible; or desires arise in him which they cease to satisfy. The result is an inward trouble to which his mind till then had been a stranger, and from which he seeks to escape by modifying his previous mass of opinions. He saves as much of it as he can, for in this matter of belief we are all extreme conservatives. So he tries to change first this opinion, and then that (for they resist change very variously), until at last some new idea comes up which he can graft upon the ancient stock with a minimum of disturbance of the latter, some idea that mediates between the stock and the new experience and runs them into one another most felicitously and expediently. This new idea is then adopted as the true one.[29]

The clash between old ideas and new experience, in short, strikes off new ideas. Experience boils over and makes us correct our present formulas. "Previous truths; fresh facts: — and our mind finds a new truth."

When anomalies accumulate to the point where old formulations are simply untenable, when the "inward trouble" of the mind becomes unbearable, innovation may come as a relief for the distraught ego and as the means to a new stability. Still new truth is characteristically a go-between, a smoother-over of transitions, marrying old opinion to new fact "so as ever to show a minimum of jolt, a maximum of continuity." For loyalty to the older truths remains a guiding principle for the psyche—so much so that "by far the most usual way of handling phenomena so novel that they would make for a serious re-arrangement of our preconception is to ignore them altogether, or to abuse those who bear witness for them."[30] We live by stereotypes; they form the picture of the world to which our habits, our capacities, our expectations have long since adjusted themselves. "No wonder, then," as Walter Lippmann has written, "that any disturbance of the stereotypes seems like an attack upon the foundations of the universe."[31] The impulse toward new ideas thus founders regularly on what James called "the obstructed will." Fresh thought, James emphasized, is inevitably *"action in the line of the greatest resistance."*[32] For creativity, however stabilizing in the longer run, may often be in the short term profoundly disorienting, disorganizing, subversive, a mortal threat to the stability of the psyche.*

Now temperaments, as James also said, determine philosophies, and always will;[33] and some people are more disposed by temperament than others to exult in change. There is an instinct for novelty as well as for routine. Emerson is plainly right in suggesting that "the party of Conservatism and that of Innovation," "the Establishment and the Movement," have "disputed the possession of the world ever since it was made."[34]

But temperamental inclination explains more why people accept new ideas than why they produce them. Here the "high motivation and persistence" noted by Simon are essential. "The typical entrepreneur," observed Schumpeter in his classic account of economic innovation, "is

---

*In this connection — though the point belongs primarily to a discussion of creativity in the arts — it is important to note Morse Peckham's persuasive argument that the function of art is precisely to combat the stereotypes, "to break up orientations, to weaken and frustrate the tyrannous drive to order, to prepare the individual to observe what the orientation tells him is irrelevant, but what very well may be highly relevant." By stimulating the essential process of disorientation, art liberates man for creation. Art "is rehearsal for those real situations in which it is vital for our survival to endure cognitive tension... is the reinforcement of our capacity to endure disorientation so that a real and significant problem may emerge.... Art is rehearsal for the orientation which makes innovation possible." Morse Peckham, *Man's Rage for Chaos: Biology, Behavior and the Arts* (Philadelphia, 1965), xi, 314.

more self-centered than other types, because he relies less than they do on tradition and connection and because his characteristic task — theoretically as well as historically — consists precisely in breaking up old, and creating new, tradition." He is not moved primarily by material or rational motives. He is rather a possessed man — possessed by "the dream and the will to found a private kingdom," by "the will to conquer... to prove oneself superior to others," and, above all, by "the joy of creating, of getting things done, or simply of exercising one's energy and ingenuity."[35]

Such motives make possible that commitment of "effort" which James thought necessary if the will was to prevail over instinctive and habitual impulse. The "strong-willed man when confronted by the novel thought," said James, "looks at its face, consents to its presence, clings to it, affirms it, and holds it fast, in spite of the host of exciting mental images which rise in revolt against it and would expel it from his mind. Sustained in this way by a resolute effort of attention, the difficult object erelong begins to call up its own congeners and associates and ends by changing the disposition of the man's consciousness altogether. And with his consciousness, his action changes, for the new object, once stably in possession of the field of his thought, infallibly produces its own motor effects."[36]

vi

It is already quite a struggle for an innovator to persuade himself to accept new ideas. But the ordeal has only begun. He must next go on to persuade others. This is an even fiercer struggle, especially in the realm of statecraft. For here majorities must be persuaded; and the resistance already overcome in the mind of the innovator returns with redoubled sodden obstinacy in the minds of the multitude. "The key to all ages," said Emerson, "is — Imbecility; imbecility in the vast majority of men, at all times, and, even in heroes, in all but certain eminent moments, victims of gravity, custom, and fear."[37]

Gravity, custom, fear — these are the powerful and perennial enemies of novelty. Opposition to changes in the cultural scheme, as Veblen said, "is instinctive, and does not rest primarily on an interested calculation of material advantages; it is an instinctive revulsion at any departure from the accepted way of doing and of looking at things—a revulsion common to all men and only to be overcome by stress of circumstances."[38] In consequence, as Machiavelli said, "There is nothing more difficult to carry out, nor more doubtful of success, nor more dangerous to handle, than to initiate a new order of things."[39]

Nor, though gravity, custom, and fear may underlie resistance to novelty, may it be concluded that such resistance is therefore always and altogether irrational. For many reasons it is better that, in society as within the individual psyche, new ideas should serve as go-betweens, smoother-overs of transition, yielding a minimum of jolt, a maximum of continuity. The social organism is too complex; drastic changes may have a train of unintended consequences; there is a limit on the capacity of mere humans to master the currents of history. "The great stream of time and earthly things," as William Graham Sumner said, "will sweep on just the same in spite of us.... It will swallow up both us and our experiments. ... That is why it is the greatest folly of which a man can be capable, to sit down with a slate and pencil to plan out a new social world." Yet even a sturdy Social Darwinist like Sumner conceded that "great discoveries and inventions," made by men, perhaps even with slate and pencil, had altered the course of the stream.[40] And such presumably wholesome innovations have the capacity, no less than absurd efforts to make the world over, to provoke mass resistance.

For change in whatever context is scary. Novelty often seems an attack on the foundations of the public as well as of the private universe. This is true of science and art—one has only to think of the ordeals of Giordano Bruno and Galileo, of Darwin and Semmelweis, of Wordsworth and Stendhal, of Joyce and Picasso — but it is preeminently the case in statecraft, where social as well as psychological threats are involved. "The reformer," as Machiavelli coolly summed up the situation, "has enemies in all those who profit by the old order, and only lukewarm defenders in all those who would profit by the new order; this lukewarmness arising partly from fear of their adversaries, who have the laws in their favour; and partly from the incredulity of mankind who do not believe in anything new until they have had actual experience of it."[41]

Profiting by the old order takes far more serious forms than making money out of it. Vested interest is protean. It may be personal—investing a mind and a career in a particular system of belief; or institutional—ideas invested in institutions become especially hard to shake; or social — investing in a system of belief that protects the power of a particular group or class. In whatever form, vested interest encourages the tendency to refuse lines of thought that are unsettling to the person, the discipline, the institution or the existing power arrangements. Vested interest thereby reinforces Emerson's citation of "the universal imbecility, indecision, and indolence of men"[42] in assuring opposition to creative statecraft. In some moods we are all Luddites.

Schumpeter's discussion of economic entrepreneurship illuminates difficulties of statecraft as well. Every step outside the boundary of routine raises doubts. The individual who ignores accustomed channels, Schumpeter noted, lacks persuasive data to justify defiance of orthodox rules of behavior. Where tradition had provided authoritative guidance, now "the success of everything depends upon intuition, the capacity of seeing things in a way which afterwards proves to be true, even though it cannot be established at the moment, and of grasping the essential fact, discarding the unessential, even though one can give no account of the principles by which this is done."[43]

The substitution of intuition for information is an inescapable hazard in creative thought. Once old frameworks are rejected, certitude gives way to conjecture. Few people are prepared to abandon cherished assumptions for admitted risks. So the very uncertainty involved in innovation strengthens the conservative instinct to play it safe and do things in the company way.

Schumpeter also emphasized the revenge taken by the social environment against those who wish to do something new. Quite apart from legal and political impediments, there is the tendency of any group to resent heresy on the part of its members. "In matters economic this resistance manifests itself first of all in the groups threatened by the innovation, then in the difficulty in finding the necessary cooperation, finally in the difficulty of winning over consumers."[44] Substitute "political" for "economic" in the first clause of this quotation, and "voters" for "consumers" in the last, and the description works as well for creative thinking in social policy.

Consider, for example, the life history of Say's Law of Markets—the proposition that supply creates its own demand and that there can therefore be no general overproduction of goods or general underutilization of resources. Malthus thought it possible, despite Say, that demand could be deficient. But he failed to establish his case, and professional economists thereafter banished the question from the literature. The issue lived on, Keynes tells us, "furtively, below the surface, in the underworlds of Karl Marx, Silvio Gesell or Major Douglas."[45]

Yet, as any fool could have seen, deficiency in demand was analytically

15

conceivable; and with the Great Depression only fools could deny the reality. Still the profession remained united in its condemnation of heresy. "Professional economists, after Malthus," as Keynes noted, "were apparently unmoved by the lack of correspondence between the results of their theory and the facts of observation; — a discrepancy which the ordinary man has not failed to observe, with the result of his growing unwillingness to accord to economists that measure of respect which he gives to other groups of scientists whose theoretical results are confirmed by observation."[46] So the ordinary citizen began to call for state intervention in the economy, while the economic profession, committed to its convenient verities, kept explaining the futility of government action till people stopped listening.

The challenge to Say's Law is only one notable instance in the intellectual history of economics where, in J. K. Galbraith's words, "economics has excluded socially inconvenient analyses, at least until some combination of pressure—the need for practical action, the social intuition of the nonprofessional, competent heresy within the profession—has upset the accepted view." And it is a "perilous matter," as Galbraith pointed out, to try and overturn cherished assumptions from within the discipline. "The jury, or most of it, is a party at interest. The fate of all who attacked Say before Keynes is a warning." The alternative—to force the issue on the discipline from without—has its perils too.[47]

What counts in the end is the subversion of old ideas by the changing environment — at least when this takes place in a society oriented to change. The Faustian societies of the West have had to greater or less degree, in H. G. Barnett's phrase a "tradition of expecting change."[48] This expectation is perhaps notably strong in the United States, but it exists generally where the idea of progress has held sway. Yet even that powerful idea has required constant validation by the environment. "It is not easy," as J. B. Bury, the historian of progress, has written, "for a new idea of the speculative order to penetrate and inform the general consciousness of a community until it has assumed some external and concrete embodiment or is recommended by some striking material evidence. In the case of Progress both these conditions were fulfilled in the period 1820 to 1850."[49] In social innovation, as in love, timing is all.

Still, while democratic societies cherish a belief in the solubility of problems and eradicability of evils, democracy may also give majorities habits of mind that strengthen resistance to alien ideas. This was not the view of democracy's early critics, who brooded much over the alleged instability of the masses and feared that popular rule would succumb to vagrant gusts of untutored opinion. But sympathetic observers like Tocqueville worried about the longer term. "What struck me in the United States," he wrote, "was the difficulty of shaking the majority in an opinion once conceived." Even when opinions became doubtful, people retained them—"not as certain, but as established"—because it took too much time and trouble to change them. "I cannot but fear," said Tocqueville, "that men [in a democracy] may arrive at such a state as to regard every new theory as a peril, every innovation as irksome toil, every social improvement as a stepping-stone to revolution, and so refuse to move altogether for fear of being moved too far."[50]

Bryce, another sympathetic observer, reached similar conclusions. The enormous force of public opinion, he felt, filled the American people "with an undue confidence in their wisdom, their virtue, and their freedom" and made public men "less eager and strenuous in striking out ideas and plans of their own, less bold in propounding those plans, more sensitive to the reproach, even more feared in America than in England, of being a crochet-monger or a doctrinaire.... In America the practical statesman is apt to be timid in advocacy as well as infertile in suggestion. He seems to be always listening for the popular voice, always afraid to commit himself to a view which may turn out to be unpopular." Bryce's hope for America was "a succession of men like the prophets of Israel to rouse the people out of their self-complacency."[51] The hope was thin. Twenty years later, even after half a dozen years of spectacular muckraking ferment, Herbert Croly noted the "many serious obstructions to any advancing intellectual movement" and called on the social critic to "stab away at the gelatinous mass of popular indifference, sentimentality, and complacency, even though he seems quite unable to penetrate to the quick and draw blood."[52]

Given the power through history of gravity, custom, and fear, the dead weight of inertia, of orthodoxy and of complacency, the tasks of persuading majorities to accept innovations remain forever formidable. Creativity in statecraft springs from the effort to resolve the intolerable tension between the imperatives of change and the vast pervasive resistance of the psyche and of society.

vii

The very magnitude of these obstacles leads some to abandon the hope of step-by-step change in favor of millennialism—the vision of the Kingdom of God, "a new heaven and a new earth," as achievable within history; the faith that would rush humanity into the ideal state by a Gestalt switch.

The argument between step-by-step and all-at-once has raged for centuries. "What we call historical development," wrote Bryce, "is really the result of a great many small expedients invented by men during many generations for curing... particular evils." A series of specific improvements, he believed, was "more likely to succeed than a large scheme, made all at once."[53] This is the distinction, given new anguish by the rise of totalitarianism, that Sir Karl Popper has made familiar to this generation—"piecemeal engineering," practical gains in the service of a broad social purpose, as against "utopian engineering" aimed at the holistic transformation of society according to a master blueprint.[54]

For Popper, Plato was the villain; perhaps true enough in a philosophical sense, though in the historical sense the millennial expectation has doubtless moved more men than *The Republic* has ever done. Millennialism claims authoritative revelation and often justifies terror in the cause of salvation. Whether the millennial passion takes religious or secular form makes little practical difference. "A fanatic," as Mr. Dooley said, "is a man that does what he thinks th' Lord wud do if He knew th' facts iv th' case."[55] People seized by faith and desperate for change tend to abandon persuasion and thereby, at least in the terms of this paper, to abandon statecraft.

Revolution—the use of violence to destroy an old political order and install a new one — may at times be the only solution for societies entrapped in hopeless logjams. Yet the resort to revolution represents, for better or worse, the failure of statecraft, nor in general is revolution a sensible weapon save *in extremis*. The passions released often overwhelm the original revolutionists, sweep society into new excesses and conclude in Thermidor. "No revolution ever carries out the programme on which it is sold to the public," Sir Denis Brogan has reminded us. "It may do more; it may do less, it will certainly do many things that its promoters do not promise and do not want. If it is really long-drawn-out and really violent, it will give magnificent opportunities to knaves, fools and monsters. Even a mild breach in orderly political development has its moral and material risks."[56] The membranes of civilization are fragile at best; once ripped asunder, they are exceedingly difficult to restore. "In a rebellion, as in a novel," as Tocqueville said, "the most difficult part to invent is the end."[57]

Absolutes are the bane of statecraft. It is the height of arrogance when frail mortals claim knowledge of the ultimate mysteries. Those who profess to execute the imperatives of God or History deceive themselves and the world. As Lincoln said, "The Almighty has His own purposes."* So does History. "Have we not," asked Hamilton in *The Federalist,* "already seen enough of the fallacy and extravagance of those idle theories which have amused us with promises of an exemption from the imperfections, weaknesses, and evils incident to society in every shape? Is it not time to awake from the deceitful dream of a golden age, and to adopt as a practical maxim for the direction of our political conduct that we, as well as the other inhabitants of the globe, are yet remote from the happy empire of perfect wisdom and perfect virtue?"[58]

The millennial hope assumes the perfectibility of man and society. Statecraft assumes rather the mixed nature of man, with decent and destructive impulses inextricably intermingled, and perceptions of good constantly foundering on the obstructed will. In an imperfect world the injunction is to attack the proximate evil today instead of demanding the absolute good tomorrow. As Woodrow Wilson used to say: Hit the head you see. "The piecemeal engineer," observed Popper, "knows, like Socrates, how little he knows." This attitude need not imply acceptance of the status quo. "A systematic fight against definite wrongs, against concrete forms of injustice or exploitation, and avoidable suffering such as poverty or unemployment," as Popper wrote, "is a very different thing from the attempt to realize a distant ideal blueprint of society. Success or failure is more easily appraised, and there is no inherent reason why the method should lead to an accumulation of power, and to the suppression of criticism. Also, such a fight against concrete wrongs and concrete dangers is more likely to find the support of a great majority than a fight

---

*Second Inaugural, March 4, 1865. He added in a letter eleven days later to Thurlow Weed, "Men are not flattered in being shown that there has been a difference of purpose between the Almighty and them. To deny it, however, ... is to deny that there is a God governing the world."

for the establishment of a Utopia."⁵⁹

The consent of the majority is essential if both the fabric of society and the freedom of the individual are to survive. To devise remedies that will both work and elicit consent is the task of creative statecraft. That task requires attention to felt human concerns rather than to alleged absolutes of God or History, as Winston Churchill observed:

> What is a short time in the history of a people, is a long time in the life of a human being. To a serene Providence a couple of generations of trouble and distress may seem an insignificant thing — provided that during that time the community is moving in a direction of a good final result. Earthly Governments however are unable to approach questions from the same standpoint. Which brings me to the conclusion that the duty of governments is to be first of all practical. I am for makeshifts and expediency. I would like to make the people who live on this world at the same time as I do better fed and happier generally. If incidentally I benefit posterity—so much the better—but I would not sacrifice my own generation to a principle — however high or a truth however great.*

---

*Winston Churchill to Bourke Cockran, April 12 [1896], Randolph Churchill, *Winston S. Churchill,* Companion Volume I, Part I (Boston, 1967), 668. Churchill's statement, made in an informal letter to an American politician, obviously requires qualification. The issue turns on the question of the certainty of foreknowledge. Most people would be willing to sacrifice small immediate benefits for large long-term benefits if they could be absolutely sure that the long-term benefits would follow. C. T. Munger suggests this example: who would prefer to lose his teeth at 50 rather than suffer the dentist every six months in the years before? Unfortunately foreknowledge of social consequences is less than foreknowledge of tooth decay. "Even with foreknowledge," Mr. Munger adds, "the problem gets more interesting when the sacrifice comes before the death of the decision-maker and the benefit comes later, i.e., to others" (personal communication, September 18, 1980).

viii

Short of the Second Coming, imperfect humanity will never reach the happy empire of perfect wisdom and perfect virtue. Still the millennial dream has its role in the dialectic of statecraft. For the revolutionary witness exposes the pretensions of and sharpens the objections to the existing order, while the revolutionary challenge undermines the weight of imbecility and vested interest. It takes statecraft to avert revolution, and the threat of revolution often facilitates the task of persuasion. Fear may suddenly become the ally rather than the enemy of peaceful change. Even the most intractable conservative, his back against the wall, may prefer reform to violence. "Since the times of Rameses," commented Henry Adams, "revolutions have raised more doubts than they solved, but they have sometimes the merit of changing one's point of view."[60]

What is preeminently true of the revolutionary threat is proportionately true of less desperate crises. In placid times masses of people are hard to move. But crisis concentrates the mind fearfully, opening it to the argument that controlled change today is better than catastrophic change tomorrow. Crisis supplies as well the incentive for creative thinking — that process, characterized by novelty, unconventionality, intense perseverance and the critical reformulation of problems, which begins with new ideas and ends in statecraft with (in Schumpeter's phrase) "the carrying out of new combinations."[61]

Establishing the new state was, after the Revolution itself, the first crisis of the American republic. The American Constitution remains an undisputed triumph of creativity in statecraft. "To evils that are common to all democratic nations," Tocqueville said of the Americans, "they have applied remedies that none but themselves had ever thought of."[62]

The Constitution represented almost a riot of institutional invention. Federalism — the division of authority between national and state governments — was, said Tocqueville, "a wholly novel theory, which may be considered as a great discovery in modern political science."[63] Federalism and judicial review, said Bryce, were "unknown to, or at any rate little used by, any previous federation."* The separation of powers among three allegedly equal and coordinate branches of government, though mistakenly ascribed by Montesquieu to the British Constitution, was in its operational workings an American innovation. "There is no medieval doctrine of the separation of powers," that most eminent of constitutional historians, Charles Howard McIlwain, has written. "... These political branches were unknown before the eighteenth century, were almost untried before the nineteenth."[64] Even the elected presidency itself was such a novel idea that the men at Philadelphia argued at length over the mode of election and the choice between a single and plural executive. Through such "new combinations" they met the problem that so much troubled Tocqueville — the preservation of liberty in an age when equality had levelled traditional barriers against despotism. They invented a polity in which ambition counteracted ambition and power checked power but which still retained the ability to act. They devised, in short, a working political system.

> Hearken not [Madison exhorted his countrymen in Federalist paper no. 14] to the voice which petulantly tells you that the form of government recommended for your adoption is a novelty in the political world;... Why is the experiment of an extended republic to be rejected, merely because it is new? Is it not the glory of the people of America, that, whilst they have paid a decent regard to the opinions of former times and other nations, they have not suffered a blind veneration for antiquity, for custom, or for names, to overrule the suggestions of their own good sense, the knowledge of their own situation, and the lessons of their own experience? To this manly spirit, posterity will be indebted for the possession, and the world for the example, of the numerous innovations displayed on the American theatre, in favor of private rights and public happiness. Had no important step been taken by the leaders of the Revolution for which a precedent could not be discovered, no government established of which an exact model did not present itself, the people of the United States... must at best have been laboring under the weight of some of those forms

---

*Bryce, *American Commonwealth*, I, 348-349. Bryce's exception referred to the Achaian League, which "had apparently a direct authority over the citizens of the several cities, but... so ill defined and so little employed that we can hardly cite that instance as a precedent." He cited no precedent for judicial review. This institution, however, was implied by the Constitution (Article VI) rather than explicitly prescribed in it.

which have crushed the liberties of the rest of mankind. Happily for America, happily, we trust, for the whole human race, they pursued a new and more noble course.... They reared the fabrics of governments which have no model on the face of the globe.[65]

The Founding Fathers had no doubt that they were undertaking an experiment, and a risky one at that. They knew their classics, and the classics had instructed them in the cycle of birth, growth, and decay that constituted the destiny of states. Their best hope, they understood, lay in their rejection of models that had failed. As Hamilton put it in the third sentence of the first Federalist paper, Americans were testing the hypothesis "whether societies of man are really capable or not of establishing good government from reflection and choice, or whether they are not forever destined to depend for their political constitutions on accident and force."[66] It was a test, they supposed, against all history. They "looked upon the new federal organization," Woodrow Wilson wrote, "as an experiment, and thought it likely it might not last."[67]

Yet the genius of the Founding Fathers lay not just in their readiness to experiment but also in their absence of illusion, their imperturbable realism and their almost unfailing sense of the balance between innovation and experience. "They were not seduced by the French fallacy," observed James Russell Lowell, "that a new system of Government could be ordered like a new suit of clothes. They would as soon have thought of ordering a suit of flesh and skin."[68] They anxiously ransacked history to find sanctions in the past, sometimes wrenched from context, that might justify boldness in the present. "They preferred," said Bryce, "so far as circumstances permitted, to walk in the old paths, to follow methods which experience had tested."[69]

True; but they did, in fact, sit down with slate and pencil in Philadelphia to plan out a new world, and with considerable success. Because of the poise they exactly maintained between prudence and experiment, between past and future, they attained a working political system. Their achievement, in Alfred North Whitehead's view, constituted one of the two occasions in history "when the people in power did what needed to be done about as well as you can imagine its being possible."[70]

The Founding Fathers, fertile as they were, did not think of everything. One thing they neglected to think of was the role in the American polity of a party system. When they thought of political parties at all, they regarded them with disfavor as prolific sources of mischief, corruption, and disunity. Yet they themselves built a contrivance that, it soon developed, could not work without parties. For only the political party could overcome the breach in the American government caused by the separation of powers and provide, in the words of the acute early student Henry Jones Ford, the "connective tissue, enfolding the separate organs" that made it possible for the executive and legislative branches to act in concert.[71]

So parties took root in the shadow of the Constitution. Like the Constitution itself, the mass political party was an American invention whose elaborate organization astonished not only Tocqueville in the 1830s but Bryce in the 1880s. The means of concert in government, parties became the means of mobilization and education in the electorate and, for a season, a means of cohesion in the nation. When the national party organization split up, so did the republic. After the Civil War the parties helped knit white America together. "The whole machinery, both of national and State governments," Bryce wrote in the 1880s, "is worked by the political parties. . . . Party association and organization are to the organs of government what the motor nerves are to the muscles, sinews, and bones of the human body. They transmit the motive power, they determine the directions in which the organs act." He added that the actual working of party government was "so unlike what a student of the Federal Constitution could have expected or foreseen, that it is the thing of all others which any one writing about America ought to try to portray."[72]

Yet the party system grew by accretion and stealth, acquired legitimacy, flourished (and now declines) without significant constitutional change.* This is often characteristic of creative statecraft in a free politi-

---

*The Twelfth Amendment involved tacit acknowledgment of the existence of parties.

cal order, especially if no palpable crisis exists of the sort that won consent to the Constitution. Even the Civil War, the most palpable of crises, was absorbed in an amended Constitution, though the Thirteenth, Fourteenth, and Fifteenth Amendments did effect sweeping changes in the old system. In less dramatic circumstances, even when perceived dysfunction demands remedy, society remains by instinct and institution conservative. Martin Van Buren and other architects of the party system did not proclaim a break with the past. The innovator within the framework characteristically proceeds with caution, rowing to his object, as John Randolph of Roanoke said of Van Buren, "with muffled oars."[73]

Machiavelli three centuries before had offered the classic statement of the predicament of reform in a society not convulsed by major crisis. "Whoever wishes to reform an existing government in a free state," he wrote, "should at least preserve the semblance of the old forms... so that it may seem to the people that there has been no change in the institutions, even though in fact they are entirely different from the old ones. For the great majority of mankind are satisfied with appearances, as though they were realities, and are often even more influenced by the things that seem than by those that are.... This rule should be observed by all who wish to abolish an existing system of government in any state, and introduce a new and more liberal one. For as all novelties excite the minds of men, it is important to retain in such innovations as much as possible the previously existing forms."[74] As Tocqueville said, "The human understanding more easily invents new things than new words."[75] Or, as Denis Brogan somewhere put it: Change everything except the appearance of things.

By respecting these principles, the American Constitution, drawn up for 4 million people living in thirteen rural provinces strung along the Atlantic seaboard, has survived with minor adjustments to embrace 230 million people living in a mighty industrial nation stretching from sea to sea and shadowing the entire planet. Vast and deep-running changes have taken place in nearly two centuries. But the semblance of the old forms is preserved — a tribute both to the wisdom with which the Founding Fathers founded and to the prudence and ingenuity with which their heirs, at the crucial moments, managed the estate.

X

The party system was one instrument of this under-the-table adjustment. Another was judicial review, with the reinterpretation of the Constitution itself permitting wider exercise of affirmative national power. The Jeffersonian tradition had begun with a bias against government in general and against the national government in particular. When each man was endowed with a sufficiency in a society of small freeholds, the role of government could only be, it was supposed, to divest the producer of the fruits of his labor. Even those merchants, bankers, and mill owners reared in the Hamiltonian tradition of the purposeful state began in time to adopt laissez-faire attitudes, especially when they discovered under Jackson that government as a weapon might be turned against them.

Then industrialization destroyed the Jeffersonian premise of property broadly distributed in a predominantly agricultural society. As economic change heaped up wealth in great agglomerations and produced a propertyless laboring class, new ways had to be found to protect the powerless from the powerful. The laissez-faire state in these new circumstances meant an abdication of democratic government before private economic power. Thoughtful observers toward the end of the nineteenth century feared the consequences for democracy. Tocqueville himself, half a century earlier, had explained "how an aristocracy may be created by manufactures" and had left the urgent warning that "if ever a permanent inequality of conditions and aristocracy again penetrate into the world, it may be predicted that this is the gate by which they will enter."[76]

Statecraft, proceeding as usual step-by-step, began to develop a strategy to defend the democratic hope. The central instrument in the new strategy was a national government drawing new powers from the Constitution. "We believe," the Populists said in their 1892 platform, "that the powers of government — in other words, of the people — should be expanded . . . to the end that oppression, injustice, and poverty shall eventually cease in the land." Theodore Roosevelt saw very clearly that, in a dynamic society of concentrated private wealth, Hamiltonian means were necessary to secure Jeffersonian ends. "Every man holds his property," Roosevelt said, "subject to the general right of the community to regulate its use to whatever degree the public welfare may require it."[77] "I feel confident," Woodrow Wilson soon added, "that if Jefferson were living in our day he would see what we see.... Without watchful interference, the resolute interference, of the government, there can be no fair play between individuals and such powerful institutions as trusts. Freedom today is something more than being left alone. The program of a government of freedom must in these days be positive, not negative merely."[78]

Both Roosevelt's New Nationalism and Wilson's New Freedom overflowed with specific political, economic, and social combinations, some better than others but the best well adapted to keep values and institutions abreast of change. It is more remarkable that the inventiveness of the Progressive Era emerged in response to what seem in retrospect only minor strains in the social organism — and a tribute to the notable leadership of Roosevelt and Wilson that in such circumstances they were able to create the taste by which their work was enjoyed. A quarter-century later the New Nationalism and the New Freedom converged at the summons of major crisis — the Great Depression — to produce the last great burst of creativity in American statecraft.

This is not to suggest that crisis infallibly calls forth creative vision. Secession did not turn Buchanan into a master of statecraft, nor depression Hoover. But in the 1930s a leader who combined courage, resourcefulness, imagination, flexibility, even deviousness, with a vigorous sense of the direction in which he wanted to carry the country came into office at a moment when a battered and bewildered people were hungry for action. Franklin Roosevelt, like T. R. and Wilson, had no doubt that the program of a government of freedom had to be positive. He could draw, moreover, on a fund of ideas developed in quieter times and now revised and extended in practical application. His eloquence against the background of despair rallied the support necessary for innovation. Some New Deal experiments were better than others, but experimentation, after all, was the way in conditions of "chronic obscurity" to discover which experiment worked and which did not. "Most action must be taken," as Henry Kissinger has noted, "when a leader cannot see his way clearly to the end."[79]

The sum of the step-by-step effort was national revival. The "new combinations," begun under the first Roosevelt and Wilson, exploding under the second Roosevelt, carried forward in later years by Truman, Kennedy, Johnson, changed America. Affirmative government civilized business and industry, made provision for the jobless and the aged, secured the rights of labor organization, assured the farmer a steady income, committed the state to the maintenance of high employment, preserved natural resources against private greed, vindicated racial justice against private bigotry, protected the Bill of Rights against private vigilantism. When Roosevelt took over in 1933, moral standards had broken down, and the machinery had stopped working. The New Deal offered new morals and machinery. The result was the attainment, for a season at least, of a working political system.

Forty years after, the question arises whether the political system still works, whether American society has not once again outgrown most of its institutions. The historian must once again perhaps put to himself the question: how long can an outworn system last?

Critics on the right insist that the idea of affirmative government is played out; that further government intervention will only make all our problems worse; that government threatens liberty and destroys self-reliance; that it is inefficient, wasteful, and corrupt; that it creates an arbitrary and obnoxious bureaucracy which exploits to its own advantage the problems it pretends to treat; that government takes on too much and miscarries through overload; that it is essentially uncreative, with no capacity to advance the goals of society.* The creative hope, such critics argue, lies in "getting government off our backs" and liberating the private energies of the economy.

Critics on the left are equally scornful, if for opposite reasons. They allege the impotence of reform, pointing out how little the New Deal and the whole step-by-step tradition have succeeded in altering the distribution of income, in reducing corporate domination of the economy, in eradicating poverty, in raising the powerless to equal status in society and in giving equal opportunities to the non-white minorities. None of these problems, they say, is soluble within a social structure organized to serve the quest for private profit.

The New Deal compromise, so to speak, seems at the point of fracture, if not of exhaustion. Where the right wants to go back to the time when private interests had clear priority over public concerns, the left wants to attempt the millennial passage into a society constructed on a radically different, if not clearly specified, set of principles. In the short run, conservatism has an advantage. "Any change in men's views as to what is good and right in human life," as Veblen said, "makes its way but tardily

---

*Cf. Jimmy Carter in his 1978 state of the union message: "Government cannot solve our problems. It can't set our goals. It cannot define our vision. Government cannot eliminate poverty, or provide a bountiful economy, or reduce inflation, or save our cities, or cure illiteracy, or provide energy."

at best.... Retrogression, reapproach to a standpoint to which the race has long been habituated in the past, is easier."⁸⁰ Meanwhile, America stands at an impasse, awaiting a new burst of creativity in statecraft.

xi

Those who have discussed the conditions of intellectual productivity," said Bryce, "have often remarked that epochs of stir and excitement are favourable, because they stimulate men's minds, setting new ideas afloat, and awakening new ambitions."⁸¹ While that is certainly true, it is also true that, in the United States at least, epochs of stir and excitement in time wear the country out and give way to epochs of apathy and drift. This inherent cyclical rhythm in our public affairs, this continuing alternation between conservatism and innovation, plainly bears upon our chances for a new outbreak of creativity in statecraft.

I inherit the cyclical perspective from my father, who presented it in 1939 in an article for the *Yale Review*.⁸² (It has held up well enough in the forty years since.) As a society, we go through seasons of action, passion, idealism, reform, and affirmative government until our energies languish. Then we long for respite and enter into seasons of withdrawal, stagnation, cynicism, hedonism, and negative government. So in the first two decades of this century two demanding presidents exhorted the American people to democratize our political and economic institutions and then to make the world safe for democracy. After twenty years of activism, the people were emotionally exhausted. They yearned for "normalcy" and elected Warren G. Harding. The politics of purpose gave way to the politics of weariness.

After the do-nothing (in a public sense) 1920s, came two more decades of action and passion — FDR and the New Deal, the Second World War, Truman and the Fair Deal, the Cold War, the Korean War — and once again the people found themselves tired and drained. So we had the Eisenhower lull in the 1950s. In due course Americans wanted to get their country moving again. As the 1920s led into the 1930s, the 1950s led into the 1960s — a new season of activism: Kennedy and the New Frontier,

Johnson and the Great Society, the racial revolution and the War on Poverty. This time desperate events gave activism a sinister turn, an edge of hysteria — first the assassination at Dallas, then the war in Vietnam. There followed riots in the cities, turmoil on the campuses, two more terrible assassinations, drugs and violence, turning on and dropping out, Watergate.... So much trauma compressed in so short a time produced exhaustion in less than the usual two decades. In the 1970s the United States became, as it had been in the 1950s and the 1920s, a spent nation, self-absorbed and cynical, the "me" decade, a people in search of rest and recuperation.

"A good deal of our politics is physiological," said Emerson.[83] Several things happen during the season of lull. The changes wrought in the previous activist period are digested by the social organism. So conservatives, who had savagely resisted the New Deal in the age of Roosevelt, accepted it in the age of Eisenhower. Moreover, the national energies begin to be replenished, the national batteries start to recharge themselves. Quietism in public life provides the opportunity for private meditation and undisturbed analysis. So the Progressive Era took off from social ideas generated in the 1890s, the New Deal from those generated in the 1920s, the New Frontier from those generated in the 1950s. Most important of all, the problems neglected in the years of cynicism and apathy become acute, threaten to become unmanageable and urgently demand remedy.

After withdrawal, return. Each period of activism has a detonating issue — a problem growing in magnitude and in menace and plainly beyond the capacity of existing ideas and institutions to control. In the early years of the century, the detonating issue was the concentration of private economic power in the trusts. In the 1930s it was depression and mass unemployment. In the 1960s it was poverty and racial justice. As the republic gathers its forces to meet such problems, it discharges energies across the board. Sometime in the 1980s, the dam will again break, as it broke at the turn of the century, in the 1930s and in the 1960s, with (we must hope) a comparable release of innovation and creativity. The detonating issues this time will no doubt be the inherent and thus far irresistible bias of the post-New Deal economy toward inflation, the movement from the industrial to the electronic era, and the passing of the age of low-cost energy — questions before which existing ideas and institutions may well be impotent.

With intelligence and courage, creative statecraft may address these problems in terms that fit the onward movement of society and may once again attain for an interval a working political system. As the velocity of history accelerates and the world hurtles on, as people tire again and want to be let off public affairs, the most recent equipoise will in time be undone. The conservatives will once again dream their dream of an idyllic past; the millenarians, theirs of the total transformation of human motives and social order.

Others may reflect with Jean Paul Sartre in the last interview before his death — Sartre who *enfin* renounced the folly of millennialism without embracing the folly of nostalgia: "I assumed that the evolution through action would be a series of failures from which something unforeseen and positive would emerge, something that was implicit in the failure but that had been overlooked by those who had hoped to succeed. That something would be a series of partial, local successes, decipherable only with difficulty by the people who were doing the work and who, moving from failure to failure, would nonetheless be achieving a certain progress. This is how I always understood history."[84]

That and the fun of trying.

Notes

1. HOBBES, LEVIATHAN, part 1, chap. 13.
2. See the useful analysis in H. G. BARNETT, *Innovation: The Basis of Cultural Change* (New York: McGraw-Hill, 1953), especially 7, 151.
3. WILLIAM WORDSWORTH, "Preface to Poems" (1815) and "Essay Supplementary to Preface" (1815) in N. C. Smith, ed., *Wordsworth's Literary Criticism* (London, H. Frowde, 1905), 150-51, 196, 198; see also ELSIE SMITH, *An Estimate of Wordsworth by His Contemporaries, 1793-1822* (Oxford: B. Blackwell, 1932).
4. *Wordsworth's Literary Criticism*, 196, 198.
5. HENRI POINCARÉ, "Mathematical Creation," *The Foundations of Science* (reprint ed., Washington, D. C., 1982), 389.
6. Preface to *The American*.
7. ANDRÉ GIDE, *Journals, 1889-1949* (Harmondsworth: Penguin, 1967), 36.
8. JAMES BRYCE, *The American Commonwealth* (London: Macmillan, 1888), 2:624.
9. HENRY KISSINGER, "Domestic Structure and Foreign Policy," in R. G. Head and E. J. Rokke, eds., *American Defense Policy* (Baltimore: Johns Hopkins University Press, 1973), 20.
10. ALEXIS DE TOCQUEVILLE, *Democracy in America*, 1, chap. 13.
11. BRYCE, *The American Commonwealth* 2:624.
12. WOODROW WILSON, *Leaders of Men*, ed. T. H. Vail Motter (Princeton: Princeton University Press, 1952), 21-22, 33.
13. Freud in "Analysis Terminable and Interminable" (1937), quoted by Janet Malcolm, "The Impossible Profession," *New Yorker*, November 24, 1980.
14. BRYCE, *The American Commonwealth* 1:31-32.
15. FRANCIS BACON, "Of Innovations," *Essays*.
16. THORSTEIN VEBLEN, *The Theory of the Leisure Class* (New York: Macmillan, 1899), chap. 8.
17. BRYCE, *American Commonwealth* 1:660.
18. ALEXIS DE TOCQUEVILLE, *The Old Regime and the French Revolution*, part 3, chap. 1.
19. HENRY ADAMS, *The Education of Henry Adams* (Boston: Houghton Mifflin, 1974), 32-33.
20. HENRY ADAMS, "The Rule of Phase Applied to History" (1909), reprinted in *The Degradation of the Democratic Dogma* (New York: Macmillan, 1919), 303.
21. ADAMS, *Education*, 53, 314.
22. ADAMS, *Education*, 107, 277, 280-81, 395.
23. JAMES MACGREGOR BURNS, *Leadership* (New York: Harper & Row, 1978), especially 4, 20.
24. BURNS, *Leadership*, 20.
25. HERBERT A. SIMON with ALLEN NEWELL and J. C. SHAW, "The Processes of Creative Thinking," in HERBERT A. SIMON, *Models of Thought* (New Haven: Yale University Press, 1979), 145.

26. J. M. KEYNES, *The General Theory of Employment, Interest, and Money* (New York: Harcourt, Brace & World, Harbinger Books, 1965), 383-84.
27. WILLIAM JAMES, "The Social Value of the College-Bred," *McClure's Magazine*, February 1908, reprinted in JAMES, *Memories and Studies* (New York: Longmans, Green and Co., 1911), 318.
28. KARL POPPER, *Unended Quest* (London: Fontana, 1976), 48.
29. WILLIAM JAMES, *Pragmatism* (New York: New American Library, Meridian reprint, 1955), 50.
30. JAMES, *Pragmatism*, 51, 145, 158.
31. WALTER LIPPMAN, *Public Opinion* (New York: Harcourt, Brace and Company, 1922), 95.
32. WILLIAM JAMES, *The Principles of Psychology* (New York: H. Holt and Company, 1890), chap. 26.
33. JAMES, *Pragmatism*, 35.
34. EMERSON, "The Conservative," "Historic Notes of Life and Letters in New England."
35. J. A. SCHUMPETER, *The Theory of Economic Development* (Cambridge: Harvard University Press, 1934), 91-93.
36. JAMES, *Principles of Psychology*, chap. 26.
37. EMERSON, "Power," in *Conduct of Life*.
38. VEBLEN, *Theory of the Leisure Class*, chap. 8.
39. NICOLO MACHIAVELLI, *The Prince*, chap. 6.
40. W. G. SUMNER, "The Absurd Effort to Make the World Over," in *Selected Essays of William Graham Sumner*, eds. A. G. Keller and M. R. Davie (New Haven: Yale University Press, 1924), 246.
41. MACHIAVELLI, *The Prince*, chap. 6.
42. EMERSON, "Napoleon, or the Man of the World," *Representative Men*.
43. SCHUMPETER, *Theory of Economic Development*, 85.
44. SCHUMPETER, *Theory of Economic Development*, 87.
45. KEYNES, *General Theory*, 32. He should have added the Americans William Trufant Foster and Waddill Catchings.
46. KEYNES, *General Theory*, 33.
47. J. K. GALBRAITH, "Economics as a System of Belief." in *A Contemporary Guide to Economics, Peace and Laughter* (Boston: Houghton Mifflin, 1971), 63, 65.
48. BARNETT, *Innovation*, 56.
49. J. B. BURY, *The Idea of Progress*, (New York: Macmillan, 1932), 324.
50. TOCQUEVILLE, *Democracy in America* 2, book 3, chap. 21.
51. BRYCE, *American Commonwealth* 2:322-23.
52. HERBERT CROLY, *The Promise of American Life* (New York: Macmillan, 1909), 451.
53. BRYCE, *American Commonwealth* 1:298.
54. KARL POPPER, *The Open Society and Its Enemies* (Princeton: Princeton University Press, 1950), 154-55.
55. [FINLEY PETER DUNNE] *Mr. Dooley's Philosophy*, (New York: R. H. Russell, 1900), 258.
56. D. W. BROGAN, *The Price of Revolution* (New York: Grosset & Dunlap, Universal Library reprint), 266-67.

57. ALEXIS DE TOCQUEVILLE, *Recollections*, chap. 5.
58. Federalist paper no. 6.
59. KARL POPPER, *The Poverty of Historicism* (Boston: Beacon Press, 1957), 67, 91-92.
60. ADAMS, *Education*, 249.
61. SCHUMPETER, *Theory of Economic Development*, 75.
62. TOCQUEVILLE, *Democracy in America* 1, chap. 17.
63. TOCQUEVILLE, *Democracy in America* 1, chap. 8.
64. C. H. MCILWAIN, *Constitutionalism: Ancient and Modern*, rev. ed. (Ithaca: Cornell University Press, 1947), 142-43.
65. Federalist paper no. 14.
66. Federalist paper no. 1.
67. WOODROW WILSON, *Constitutional Government in the United States* (New York: Columbia University Press, 1908; reprint ed., New York: Columbia University Press, 1961), 44-45. For a discussion of these issues, see ARTHUR SCHLESINGER, JR., "America: Experiment or Destiny?" *American Historical Review*, June 1977.
68. JAMES RUSSELL LOWELL, "Address on Democracy" (1884), quoted in BRYCE, *American Commonwealth* 1:31.
69. BRYCE, *American Commonwealth* 1:31.
70. LUCIEN PRICE, ed., *Dialogues of Alfred North Whitehead* (Boston: Little, Brown, 1954), 161, 203. The other occasion was the age of Augustus.
71. HENRY JONES FORD, *The Rise and Growth of American Politics* (New York: Macmillan, 1898), 215.
72. BRYCE, *American Commonwealth* 5:636-37.
73. WILLIAM CABELL BRUCE, *John Randolph of Roanoke* (New York: G. P. Putnam's Sons, 1922), II, 203.
74. MACHIAVELLI, *Discourses on Livy*, book 1, chap. 25.
75. TOCQUEVILLE, *Democracy in America* 1, chap. 8.
76. TOCQUEVILLE, *Democracy in America* 2, book 2, chap. 20.
77. THEODORE ROOSEVELT, *The New Nationalism* (New York: The Outlook Company, 1910), 23-24.
78. WOODROW WILSON, *The New Freedom* (New York: Doubleday, Page, & Company, 1913), 284.
79. Interview with HUGH SIDEY, *Time*, October 20, 1980.
80. VEBLEN, *Theory of the Leisure Class*, chap. 8.
81. BRYCE, *American Commonwealth* 2:623.
82. ARTHUR M. SCHLESINGER, "Tides of American Politics," *Yale Review*, December 1939.
83. "Fate" in *Conduct of Life*.
84. BENNY LÉVY, "The Last Words of Jean-Paul Sartre," *Dissent*, Fall 1980, 403.

The Council of Scholars
of the Library of Congress

1980-1982

Daniel J. Boorstin
The Librarian of Congress

Jaroslav J. Pelikan
Chair

Meyer H. Abrams
Class of 1916 Professor of English
Cornell University

James S. Ackerman
Professor of Fine Arts
Harvard University

Saul Bellow
Raymond and Martha Hilpert
  Gruner Distinguished Service
  Professor of English
University of Chicago

Paul Berg
Sam, Lula and Jack Willson
  Professor of Biochemistry
Stanford University

Daniel J. Boorstin
The Librarian of Congress

Subrahmanyan Chandrasekhar
Morton D. Hull Distinguished
  Service Professor of
  Astrophysics
University of Chicago

Philip D. Curtin
Professor of History
The Johns Hopkins University

Elizabeth Eisenstein
Alice Freeman Palmer Professor of
  History
University of Michigan

Leopold Ettlinger
Professor of History of Art
University of California at Berkeley

Gerald Holton
Mallinckrodt Professor of Physics
  and Professor of History of
  Science
Harvard University

Henry Kissinger
Secretary of State, 1973-1977

Maxine Kumin
Consultant in Poetry
Library of Congress, 1981-1982

Archibald MacLeish
Poet, Librarian of Congress,
  1939-1944

Myres S. McDougal
Sterling Professor of Law, Emeritus
Yale University

Yehudi Menuhin
Violinist, Conductor, Musicologist

William Meredith
Consultant in Poetry
Library of Congress, 1978-1980

Jaroslav J. Pelikan
Sterling Professor of History and
  Religious Studies
Yale University

Ernest Samuels
Franklin Bliss Snyder Professor of
  English, Emeritus
Northwestern University

Arthur M. Schlesinger, Jr.
Albert Schweitzer Professor of
  Humanities
City University of New York

JOHN HOPE FRANKLIN
James B. Duke Professor of History
Duke University

JACOB W. GETZELS
R. Wendell Harrison Distinguished
    Service Professor of Education
University of Chicago

NATHAN GLAZER
Professor of Education and Social
    Structure
Harvard University

CHAUNCY D. HARRIS
Samuel N. Harper Distinguished
    Service Professor of Geography
University of Chicago

CARL SCHORSKE
Professor of History
Princeton University

THEODORE W. SCHULTZ
Charles L. Hutchinson
    Distinguished Service Professor
    of Economics
University of Chicago

EDWARD G. SEIDENSTICKER
Professor of Japanese
Columbia University

COUNCIL MEMBERS, ELECTED MAY 1982

LAWRENCE A. CREMIN
President
Teachers College
Columbia University

CLIFFORD J. GEERTZ
Professor, School of Social Science
Institute for Advanced Study

ANTHONY HECHT
Consultant in Poetry
Library of Congress, 1982-1983

EDITH KERN
Doris Silbert Professor in the
    Humanities
Smith College

ROBERT NOZICK
Professor of Philosophy
Harvard University

EDMUND D. PELLEGRINO
John Carroll Professor of Medicine
    and Medical Humanities
Georgetown University

J. G. A. POCOCK
Professor of History
Johns Hopkins University

EMILY VERMEULE
Professor of Classics
Harvard University

RESIDENT SCHOLARS, 1981-1982

JUAN FERRANDO BADÍA
Vice Rector
University de Alcalá de Henares

VICENTA CORTÉS
Inspector General
The Archives of Spain

JINICHI KONISHI
Professor of Japanese Literature
University of Tsukuba

JULIÁN MARÍAS
Professor of Philosophy
University of Madrid

LIBRARY OF CONGRESS OFFICERS

JOHN C. BRODERICK
Assistant Librarian for Research
    Services

JAMES H. HUTSON
Executive Secretary
Council of Scholars